THE DOONESBURY CHRONICLES

Doonesbury Books in Holt Paperback Editions

THE DOONESBURY CHRONICLES
G. B. Trudeau
With an Introduction by Garry Wills

Holt, Rinehart and Winston/New York

10 9 8 7 6 5 4 3 2

You could be laughing at me,
You've got the right.
But you go on smiling...
                              —Jackson Browne

Introduction by Garry Wills

Almost every one of us so-called adult male Americans is a jock manqué. We only decided to be above all that the time when it dawned on us we were just not good enough for the pros—or even for the midget team. (My own basketball was played on a humiliatingly submidget team called "The Mosquitos.") For a while, there was a consolation prize. Perhaps stardom was out of reach; but one might still become the obviously next-best-thing, a sports *announcer*. In fact, we had already been that in all our daydreaming of stardom. What good is it to knock out a ghostly home run, or dunk a phantom basketball, if the world does not hear of it and shout approval? So watch boys dribbling on a downtown asphalt court or cuffing balls across a sandlot—you will, in time, trace an odd antiphonal pattern of sportscasters "announcing" each boy's game. "Here comes Denny the Dunk up the court, making fantastic moves," Denny reports to the tiered thousands of invisible Denny-fans.

And Lenny, covering him, has his own announcer: "But Slick Lenny has him all sewed up—and almost steals the ball! What hands!" Almost every boy who ever dabbled in sports has spent hours being three things all at once—performer, announcer, and fan. It is one of the basic exercises in that shared human trait of watching, judging, and approving (or groaning at) one's own activity. Chesterton once said that we are the only laboratory specimens that study themselves through a microscope that *is* ourselves.

In 1968 the Yale *Daily News* featured a cartoon strip by an undergraduate named Garry Trudeau. The Yale football team's star quarterback at the time was Brian Dowling, and one way to deflate the superstar back to the general level of us duffers and misfits was to imagine him still doing the internal patter of adulation long after he had acquired a real announcer to celebrate his feats. So there goes big Number Ten, "B.D.," into the huddle—he calls the play as if he were announcing it during the execution: "I fade back to our own five-yard line. Waiting until at least three men are upon me, balancing on one foot, I throw an underhand ninety-five-yard spiral, which I'll run down and catch on the goal line."

But it is even more satisfying to imagine the great B.D. off the field, announcing other kinds of games that all men play. Here he is at a college mixer, beginning to socialize: "While he coolly sips on his ginger ale, the young college quarterback awaits the rush which will undoubtedly come when word gets out that he is here at Briarcliff . . . ." And, just in case they don't recognize him, B.D. is still wearing his football helmet. (Later, of course, B.D. the all-American jock will go to Vietnam and wear that same helmet instead of the military kind—the white Yale helmet even gets autographed by Bob Hope after one of his Christmas shows.)

If it is fun to dream of a successful jock still dreaming of becoming a successful jock, it is even better to watch B.D.'s klutzy roommate, Mike Doonesbury, "announcing" his miserable performances: "Mike 'the Mix,' inexperienced but eager freshman, still looks around for his first score of the evening"—only to be addressed finally as "you gross, skinny frosh." Always, of course, Trudeau's characters give themselves their own sports nicknames, which tend to become ludicrous in other people's mouths. Doonesbury cheers himself on as "Mike the Mix" and "Mike the Man." Mark Slackmeyer, campus radical, comes before us to seize the university president's home: "With discontent in the air, the SDS has staged a rally in front of the president's house, led by 'Megaphone' Mark." Unfortunately for the Megaphone, others reduce him to scale by using the silly diminutive "Megs." You can't win if you're a Trudeau character.

Even the president of Yale, Kingman Brewster, plays sports announcer to his own performance in the campus wars: "It's more kudos for Yale's Youthful President as he starts out on his morning walk through the colleges to reduce tension." But while he preens himself abroad, Slackmeyer has seized his home.

Jim Andrews, of the Universal Press Syndicate, found Trudeau's strip in the *Daily News* and asked to syndicate it commercially. He was repaid, later in their friendship, by entering the strip as an oil magnate during the 1974 gasoline shortage. At first Trudeau just slightly recast his old situations to fit every campus and the family newspapers: The "Y" got scrubbed off B.D.'s helmet, naked girls in the dorms got their clothes put back on, and swear words disappeared. But Trudeau's world opened up when he got into the realm of politics. Despite Megaphone Mark's rallies, and Mike's inept drags on a marijuana joint, there had been only one strip of real political satire in the Yale days—when B.D. so cowed and abused his replacement in a huddle that the rest of the team called the underdog "Hubert."

All that changed in the extraordinarily successful commercial strips from which this book is assembled: B.D. went to war, and Mike started tutoring in the ghetto, and Joanie Caucus ran away from her husband and children to be liberated. Mark even dragged Mike off to a peace march in Washington, where Mike argued with Joe Alsop while Mark called on Vice-President Humphrey (heard still trying to spell his name over the phone to President Nixon).

Yet the world that Trudeau entered remained close to his basic insight. Send B.D. to Vietnam, where he gets captured, and his captor will introduce himself to an inaudible ringside cheer: "Who ain't heard of Phred the Terrorist?" Phred, it turns out, is just joining the family business—his father pressured him into the firm. Zonker Harris, the flowery freak-out who tends Walden Puddle, goes to Vietnam to cover B.D.'s exploits in sportscasts from the front. The coffee-house priest introduces himself in the third person, and with reference to his clips: "The fighting young priest who can talk to the young . . . Birmingham, Selma, Chicago '68." A ghetto tour is conducted as if for television. Jeb Magruder's penitence becomes an "In Concert" traveling show. Everything is "covered" as a sports event.

During the Senate Watergate hearings, Megaphone Mark took a job as a disc jockey and became "Marvelous Mark," playing Watergate profiles as personal-request numbers: "Okay! Profile on John Dean III going out to Joey with hugs from Donna!" When Trudeau had Mark conclude his judicious profile on John Mitchell by doing an ecstatic jig to cries of "Guilty, guilty, guilty!" the Washington *Post* killed the strip and editorialized: "We cannot have one standard for the news pages and another for the comics." I agree. How can the rest of us journalists ever live up to Trudeau's standards?

The sportscaster technique even served Trudeau in the least likely connection—his affectionate portrait of the "libber" Joanie Caucus. Billie Jean King helped, of course. Ms. Caucus and women's sports arrived simultaneously in the day-care center: "We can't *all* wear tennis dresses with blue sequins. Basically, it's just not possible. Anyway, I'm thinking of changing to Margaret Mead." That last sentence shows us why the self-announcing trait of Trudeau's characters is not limited to males or to jocks. Joanie's day-care children are only liberated by taking on role-models—"B.J." King, or Ms. Mead, or Joanie herself. And even Joanie can only break the mold of what she is "supposed" to be by taking up a publicly defined role—"women's libber," a type delivered to her in the newspapers. She is testing her "game" against Betty Friedan's, as surely as the sandlot kid is re-enacting a Ted Williams performance.

Trudeau's way of making characters deliver a running commentary on their own acts, a commentary cast in the third person, opens up that inner space in which personality can grow. We think too often of "playing a role" as something artificial, at odds with reality. But we are all role-players, to our roots. We become by pretending. We feign humanity. We must "play" child before we get a chance to "play" adult—and in both cases we are quietly watching and indulgently grading (even while fearing or resenting) our own performance. The process of growth is in large part a willingness to risk new roles—something Joanie perfectly exemplifies in her breakout. She runs away on Mark's motorbike long after she should have "settled down" in her one role as wife-mother. B.D. kids Mike when the cyclists arrive back at the commune with Joanie: "Little of the ol' Mrs. Robinson, eh, Mikey?" But Joanie, getting on toward Mrs. Robinson's age, is more like the kids in *The Graduate*. Except that her breakout is both more difficult and more realistic—she is rushing off to find a job, not to escape one. In fact, eventually she will be "A Graduate"—a new role for her—if Berkeley's law school survives her incursion. And meanwhile she teaches not only her day-care charges, but her young friends in the commune as well.

Humor is always complex and precarious—the Real's nervous *j'accuse* hurled at the Ideal, in the name of the Ideal. That is why the humor that ultimately fails is the kind that does not take itself seriously enough—without the risk, there is no joke. And a humor that has Trudeau's starting point makes its own complexity the point. Mike at the mixer *is* what he bills himself as: "Inexperienced but eager freshman" looking around for his first score. But that hardly makes him "Mike the Mix." Still, he must try to be Mike the Mix in order to stand his ground at all, to keep from running away. We all only pretend to be heroes—even our heroes. (That is what B.D. is all about.)

Trudeau's characters are watching each other watch themselves, just like the rest of us. We travel toward ourselves by detours only. We grow not so much by addition as by division—and multiplication. The more "things" we are, the more roles we have tried, the more we become a unique and united self. The "simple" man is less than a man, and much of a corpse. The complex man is an army on the move. That is why Trudeau's kind of talking-to-oneself is the only way, finally, to communicate with others.

Trudeau's approach has a very practical effect on his strip. Since his characters are caught in the process of defining themselves over-against some public role, they have no trouble moving out, anywhere, into the world. Mark can as easily talk to Hubert Humphrey as to Brian Dowling or to "King" Brewster. That is not as common an ability as one might think in today's "funnies," which have by and large tended a small "lyrical" garden and an inner world. "Peanuts" is as good an example as any: Its world is a playground uncontaminated by adults, or even by the clothes, furniture, or reminders of adults. The strip says that we are all children; there are no adults. That view has just enough truth in it to get by, but the strip does so by a drastic narrowing. The fantasy-for-its-own-sake ends up logically in a dog's dream of being a German air-ace. This is not role-playing as a way of trying on a world to see if it fits, but as a way of escaping the world. Happiness is a toy puppy's nose. Much the same thing can be said of Broom Hilda's blasted heath, or Pogo's later (desiccating) swamp. Al Capp kept his strip alive so long because Abner could leave Dogpatch and go to Washington, or to Lower Slobbovia. When Walt Kelly dragged Joe McCarthy and Spiro Agnew into the swamp, that upset its ecology forever. The more interesting characters, like Miz Mam'selle Hepzibah and Porky Pine, began to lose their particular reality.

The natural terminus of this shrinking "inner world" of comedy is the solipsism of Jules Feiffer's characters, who pursue themselves expressionlessly through panel after panel and crumble when they catch themselves. Trudeau has obviously learned from Feiffer; he uses repeated panels with little or no visual change to indicate thought processes going on *behind* a façade. But Feiffer's characters are stranded in a desert of themselves, while Trudeau's people interact. Indeed, it is when he is superficially most like Feiffer that the difference becomes clearest.

Richard Nixon is a voice coming out of the TV set, that just sits there for panel after panel. Then, at the end, even klutzy Mike Doonesbury's head drops in embarrassment for the overreacher's last mendacity. The "Nixon" portrayed here—or, rather, studiously left unportrayed—is not the historian's Nixon, or the journalist's. He is the Nixon whose voice enters Walden Puddle's commune and makes its residents react. He is the Nixon B.D. praises when others wonder how the man kept a silly war going so long: "The President is a lot smarter than you think."

So Trudeau, despite his sketchy and Feifferesque economy of drawing, has brought narrative back to the *funny* strips (as opposed to inked-in soap operas), where it has been missing since the great days of Capp's schmoos and kygmies. B.D.'s capture by Phred gave Trudeau a way to arch a single story over several weeks while keeping each segment funny. And we have to keep reminding ourselves of the truly astonishing achievement this represents—that he made us laugh at the Vietnam war during its most corrosive stages. Trudeau's Vietnam was, to the late sixties, what Capp's Slobbovia was to the Cold-War forties.

Yet the war strips in Vietnam were not the toughest challenge Trudeau set for himself. For that prize I would nominate the tour de force of Phred's visit to Washington, accompanied by three hundred refugees disguised as Coca-Cola (*they're* the real thing). You have to remember the story (a sign of the characters' strength): Phred, to keep the sports-star analogy alive, was up for renewal of his terrorist contract; but he was asking too much—his mother wanted a fresh motorbike for her *plastiqueuse* getaways. So Phred gets traded to another team (the Pathet Lao). After tiring of the scenery in Laos (mainly refugees as far as the eye can see), he took a tourist flight to beautiful Cambodia, where most of the briefly remaining scenery was also refugees. He asked an oriental Grant Wood couple (complete with pitchfork) if their museum was destroyed in the secret Cambodian bombings:

"*Secret* bombings? . . . I remarked on them. I said, 'Look, Martha, here come the bombs.'"

"It's true, he did."

That set up the situation. Then Trudeau launched four weeks of strips that brought homeless refugees to Washington as congressional witnesses. (They fly in on a plane returning empty Coke bottles to keep a ruined Cambodia beautiful.) Hunger and tragedy yield a weird music of laughter. The hearings, needless to say by now, get "announced" as a quiz show: Who can identify a phantom jet while being bombed by it? What *prizes* for the witnesses? Mike watches the hearings at home. Though he is B.D.'s old roommate, he has not (yet) met Phred. It is a large world Trudeau has taken to roaming in; and only we, the readers, are let into all parts of it.

It is surprising that politics freed Trudeau for these wanderings. The political animals that entered Okefenokee contaminated it, and the later humor of "Li'l Abner" crumpled under a kind of political hatred. Capp's Joanie Phoney was not only less fair than Joanie Caucus, from a political point of view, she was just less funny. Ms. Caucus is not an anti-Phoney. The reason is, again, Trudeau's creative interplay of the self against its roles. Though the satire has bite, it remains surprisingly kindly. There are no really hateful characters in the strip—not even the pilots who casually erase entire countries under their wing-tips while discussing a Knicks game. Mark, the radical, is not hated—and neither are the hard hats who beat him up. Some might consider Phred the acid test—what other artist could make a terrorist amiable? Not even the Watergate criminals were treated with unbridled bitterness. Not even Nixon, who was presented as a kind of Dagwood under his various imperial roles; all the evil demands he made upon himself and could not, mercifully, meet. The most moving cartoon on the President's resignation showed the demolition of a brick wall that grew up around the White House in earlier strips. It seemed more like the freeing of a prisoner than the storming of a bastille.

Over and over Trudeau affects a neat, almost surgical division between indignation and malice. Usually only sanctity can make such hairline incisions; but comedy, too, is a thing of rigor and discipline, a kind of secular asceticism (ask the best of them, Mark Twain). Trudeau's characters fail and bumble themselves into our affection. It is one thing to laugh at a klutz; it is another thing entirely to laugh at a man who is obviously mocking himself for being a klutz. He has co-opted us, this Doonesbury. We laugh with him, in a camaraderie of klutziness. "Mike the Man" is silly. But ridicule only deflates him to "Mike, a Man"—and there is no higher earthly title. Trudeau always sees a person *under* the roles, struggling with them. His wisdom mocks forgivingly, and each target of his ridicule is haloed with laughter's benediction.

Author's Preface:

Four years four months gone by, and I find myself ready to embark on what is shaping up to be an arduous fact-finding mission to Pago Pago, which is, at least this year, the seat of government in American Samoa. Yes, it has come to that. In the event that for one reason or another I don't survive the crossing of the international date line, I must make my peace and leave behind these cryptic notes, with the hope that they will ultimately find their way into the comprehensive retrospective now in the making.

I have just finished reading an astonishingly well-reasoned critique of "Doonesbury," written and sent to me by Alice, age eight, president of a Tallahassee chapter of the Sunshine and Smiles John Denver Fan Club. The letter is filled with angry words for me, for I have slighted her idol in some recent strips, and, as I have learned this past month, hell hath no fury like that of a fan of John Denver scorned. Nonetheless, for all its excesses, the letter seems to me particularly forthright, written with an urgency and directness that invariably characterize the communications of the very young. Walt Kelly, creator of "Pogo," used to believe that cartoonists should be attended at all times by staffs of small, insouciant children in whose wisdom and vision he correctly placed absolute faith. To see through the essentially egalitarian eyes of a child, where nothing escapes notice and everything starts out with an equal importance, is to celebrate the boundless, shimmering diversity of everyday experience. The young seem to reach out to grasp *all* of life's perceptual confetti: colors and cues, sights and sounds, notions of every sort are permitted wondrous entry. Nothing is ignored and nothing is wasted. With wobbly logic and earnest assumptions, children are free to order their priorities more or less randomly; only later are they taught that the blackboard is more important than the wall that frames it.

The rest of us can only envy from afar this tumbled but guileless universe. As the naturalist Annie Dilliard lamented, "I would like to know grasses and sedges—and *care*. Then my least journey into the world would be a series of happy recognitions." And happy recognitions, no matter how seemingly common, are the stuff from which the dreams and fantasies of children are conjured. Nothing else is required. In the quintessential cartoon fantasy of Slumberland in Winsor McCay's "Little Nemo," a small boy dropped off to sleep and the tiniest objects of his day were transformed into the wondrous vehicles of his nights. In his dreams, Nemo floated on a milkweed seed, toppled from a colossal mushroom, and was whisked away in an ivory coach drawn by cream-colored rabbits. The scale of the objects corresponded to the importance that the boy attached to them—hence, giant raspberries and miniature furniture. Through it all, the value of

Slumberland established itself through its contribution to the child's experience, and when the excitement of the vision deposited him, as it always did, in a jumble of sheets on the hardwood floor beside his bed, it was only the artist's implicit assurance that Nemo would have other dreams to explore that kept away the disappointment.

A flight of fantasy, whether in dream or daydream, is no mere sleight of mind. But only children will accept it as being equally as profound as the arbitrary state of awareness we are taught to regard as reality, and hence, only they are nurtured by it. Later, of course, many of us comprehend our self-imposed poverty and try to double back, but the bread crumbs are always missing and our failures are immense. A true belief in the validity of nonordinary reality—with all that it can teach us—seems beyond the capabilities of every practicing adult, with the possible exception of Federico Fellini.

Perhaps this sad state of affairs helps explain the indispensable function of the cartoonist in society. When he's doing his job, he provides us with the means to look back into ourselves; he's the benign conduit between our self-serious façades and those pockets of vulnerability buried deep within. The challenges he negotiates are considerable: to create a compelling fantasy—whether Slumberland or Okefenokee—and to invite the reader to involve himself in a new reality set up as a sustained metaphor for his own; to let the small meannesses and foolishnesses of life face each other in distortion, stretched, juggled, and juxtaposed, but always lit with laughter to ease the pain of self-recognition; to seek out the vignette that speaks much to the lives of many; to distill and refine language so as to epitomize, and to look everywhere for simple meanings—even in the grasses and sedges. These are the purposes of the precious few in this business who have really meant something to their readers; the purposes of artists who had the capability of endowing a given strip with such exquisite flow of allusion that one almost expected it to lift like a decal and float off the page.

As many of the cartoons in this collection amply demonstrate, there are myriad places to go wrong. In what is unavoidably a chronicle of one's own personal maturation, self-indulgence and contrivance abound. And in the pursuit of tomfoolery the desire to join battle sometimes overwhelms. Yet, in more thoughtful moments, I have tried to observe Kelly's famous advice of almost twenty years ago: "There is no need to sally forth, for it remains true that those things which make us human are, curiously enough, always close at hand. Resolve, then, that on this very ground, with small flags waving, and tiny blasts of tinny trumpets, we have met the enemy, and not only may he be ours, he may be us."

Garry Trudeau
New Haven, Connecticut
February 26, 1975

I/High Tides and Greener Grass

It wasn't just Mark Slackmeyer on a proletariat lark, taking a hard-hat job over summer vacation—*everybody* was just dying to establish a dialogue. If you were a college professor, it might help to bring in for your class an actual Black Panther, or offer a course in Consciousness 10-A. Even better if you were a fighting young priest who could talk to the young. Still, communications could be requited, or unrequited, on more fundamental planes: Doonesbury working on his timing at fraternity mixers, Mark's father trying to tune in on his son via "Mod Squad," and B.D. turning from the frustrations of the huddle to the invigorating, simpler pleasures of combat training. Everything, if not everyone, seemed poised.

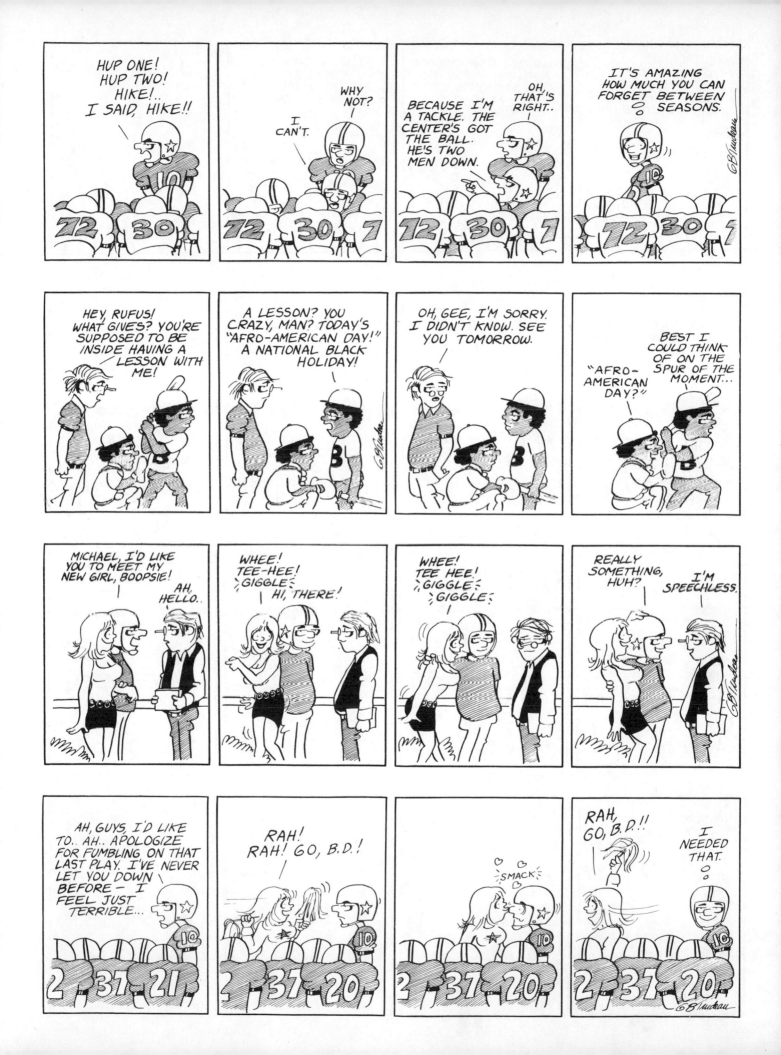

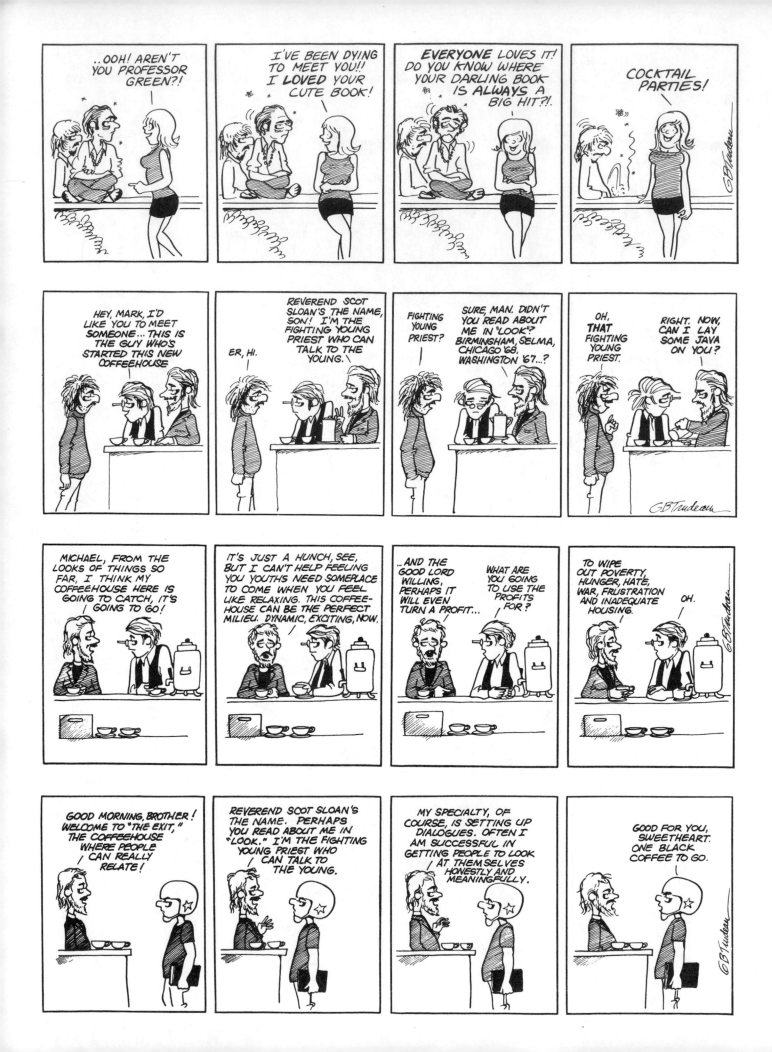

II/The Sounds of Falling Dominoes

There was—had been, would be—a war. "To the 'Nam," B.D. called to his MATS pilot, and indeed there was a certain piquancy to life at Firebase Bundy, though it hardly prepared one for the likes of a Vietcong terrorist named Phred. On the home front a farmer could warble ". . . sweet land of subsidy," and the more callow slackards could huddle in communes. Some, like Zonker, could fall in love with a wheat patch. But the country out there, however schizophrenic, was too big to be ignored, at least so Mike and Mark must have reasoned before setting out on a transcontinental fact-finding motorcycle tour, an odyssey that netted them one runaway housewife. And if Joanie Caucus could turn her life around, so could . . . Zonker get a job as a mailman, the Reverend Scot Sloan go dating, and hard-headed B.D. see what the war was all about in stunned reunion with his pal the terrorist. Lines of sight were adjusting.

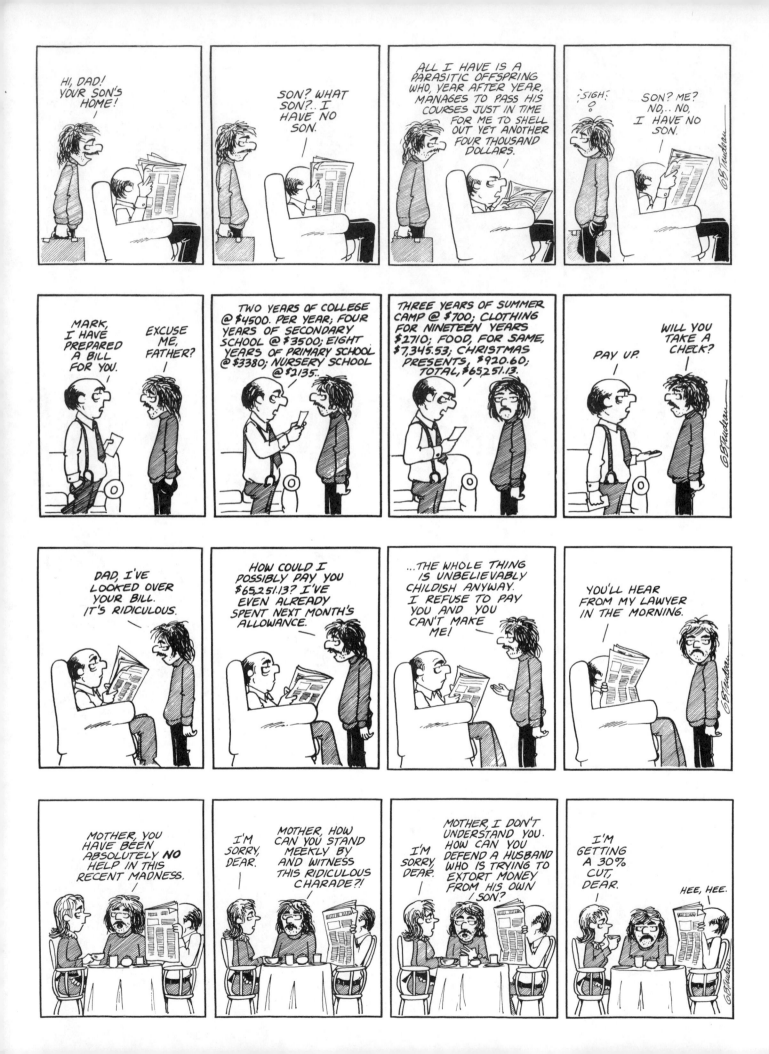

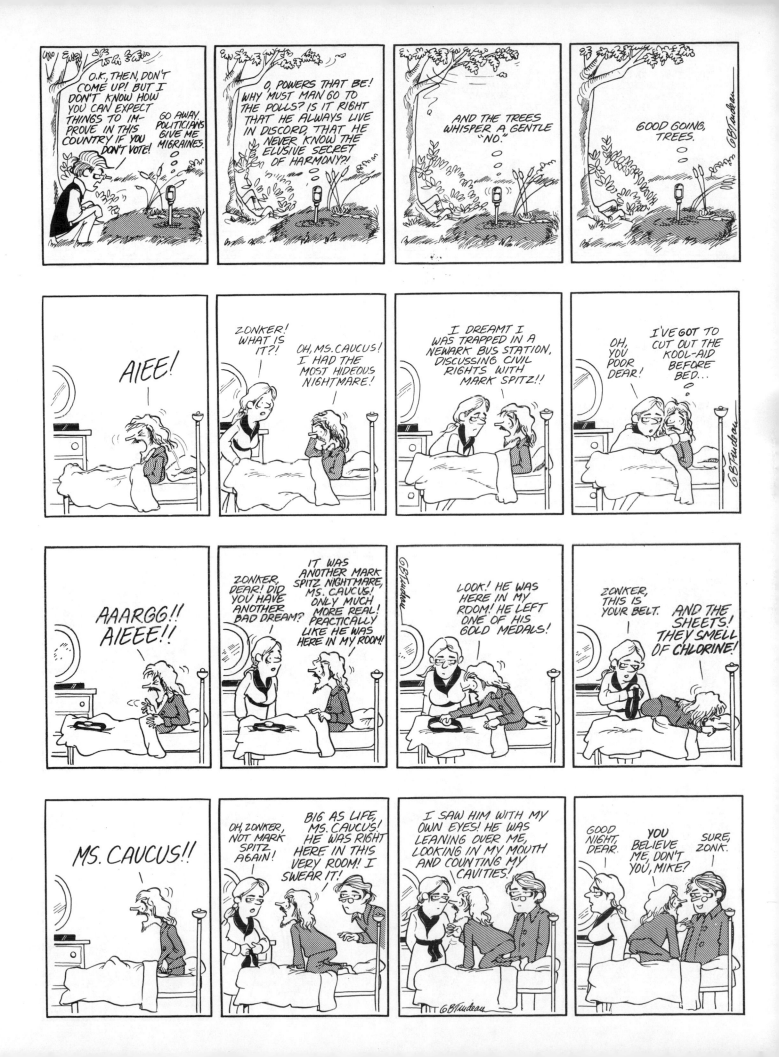

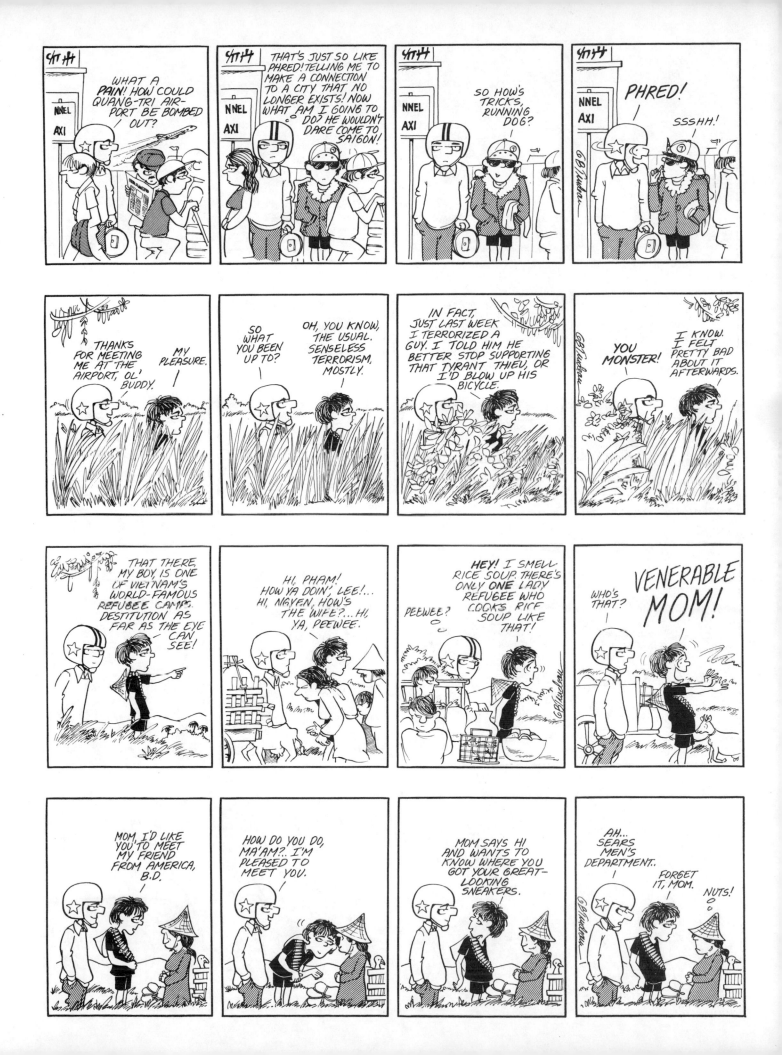

III/A Lasting Piece of the Action

Disengagements become rife, with mixed blessings for the disengaged. Phred, on his own now, finds himself traded to the Pathet Lao, but seeing the ghost of America haunting almost all of Indochina, he is inspired to return the memories by organizing an airlift of homeless Cambodians to Washington, allowing liberal congressmen, and even Georgetown matrons, to adopt their very own refugees. But before patronization comes recrimination—whether at the White House, toiling in the coils of Watergate, on the lecture circuit with a flamboyantly penitent Jeb Magruder, or the more traditional mumblings at the class of '43 reunions. All such turns and pangs are witnessed bucolically by the denizens of Walden Commune, though not without contributions of their own—such as Mark taking to the airwaves as a DJ with Watergate profiles ("Guilty, guilty, guilty!"), and Joanie working wonders at the day-care center in extracting sexism from her scruffy charges.

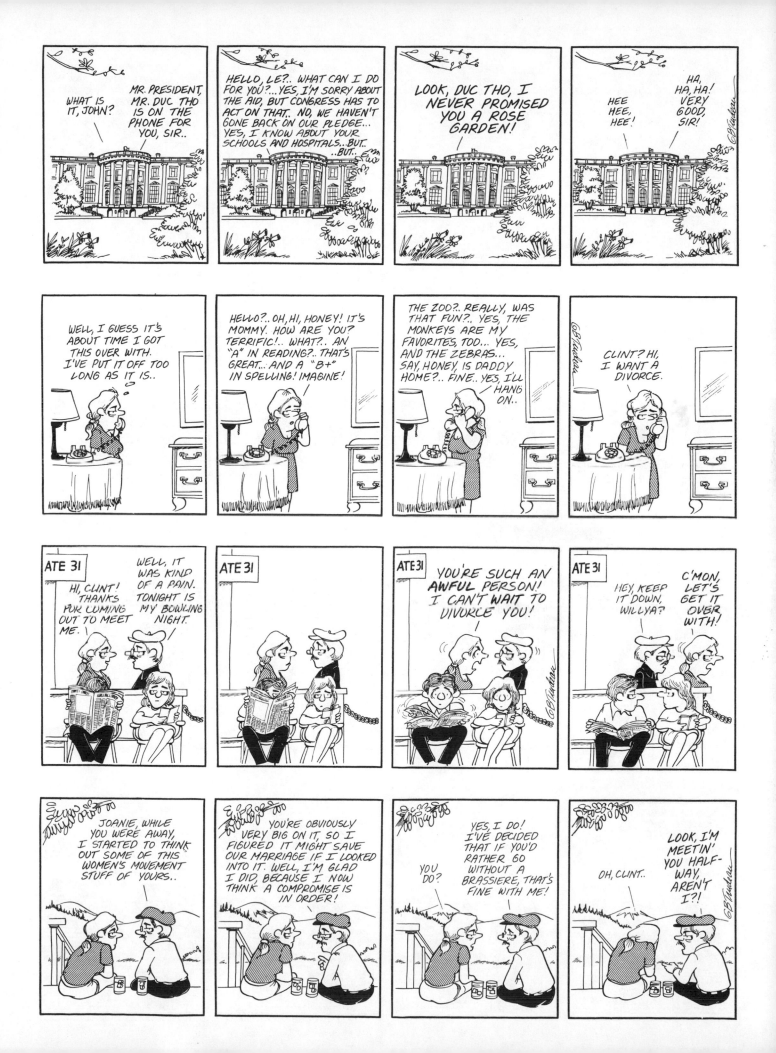

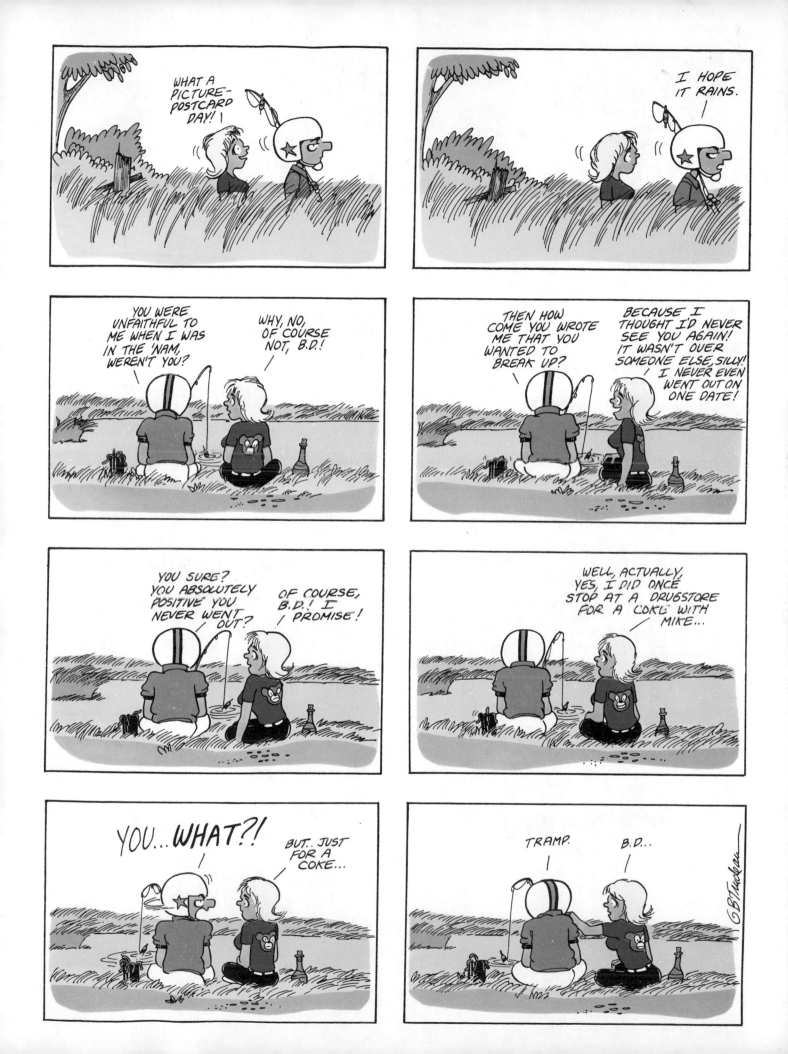

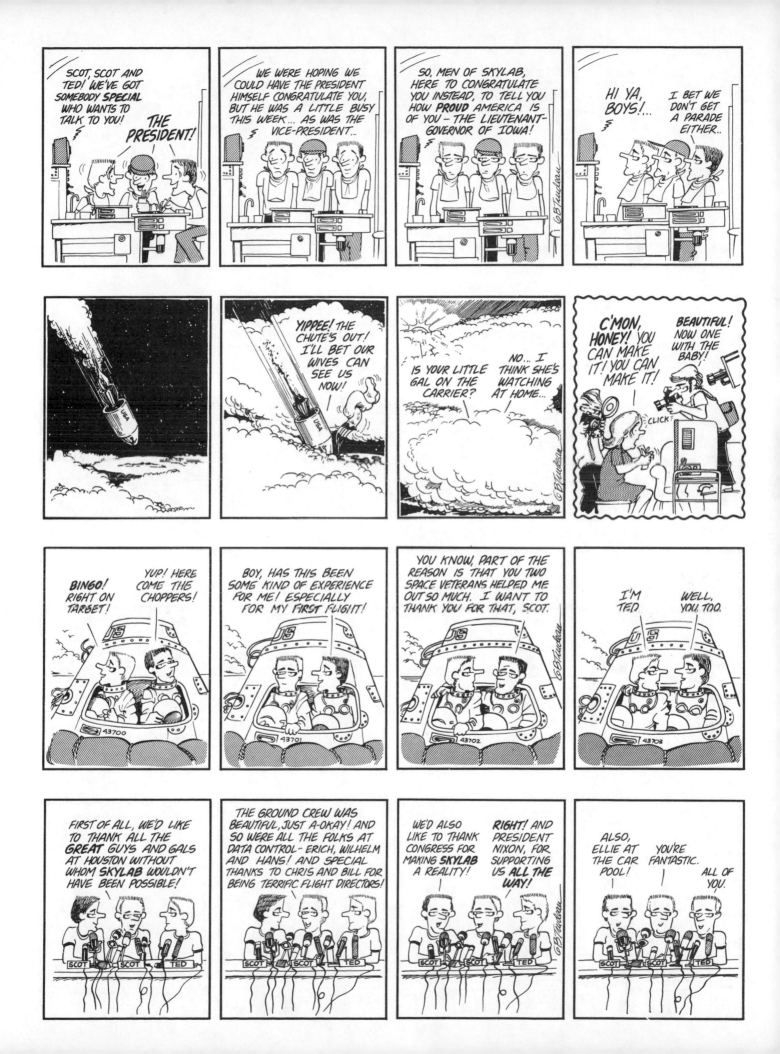

IV/Tripping Down the Hangout Route

Our passion for instant nostalgia would seem inexhaustible and cunning, especially in times of crisis. Taking two widely disparate cases in point, we have the Watergate Many reuning over Mrs. Dean's onion dip and serenading themselves as "Richard Nixon's Secret Tapes Club Band," while that other crisis, the one affecting everybody's gas tank, finds Mark Slackmeyer dusting off his revolutionary regalia preparatory to coaching some discontent truckers in the art of confrontation. And at the eyes of the two storms, things are positively medieval—as Fort Nixon digs in for the good of future Presidents, and the Energy Czar calls for hot wax and signet ring to allocate an extra five gallons for a mother's son forced to live two months at a turnpike Hot Shoppe. But *Time* marches on—indeed, it sends a totally credulous reporter to interview Zonker on "The New Hedonism"—and a few souls work to nobler purposes, though Joanie finds the road to law school more than a little rocky. But there are many ways to stonewall.

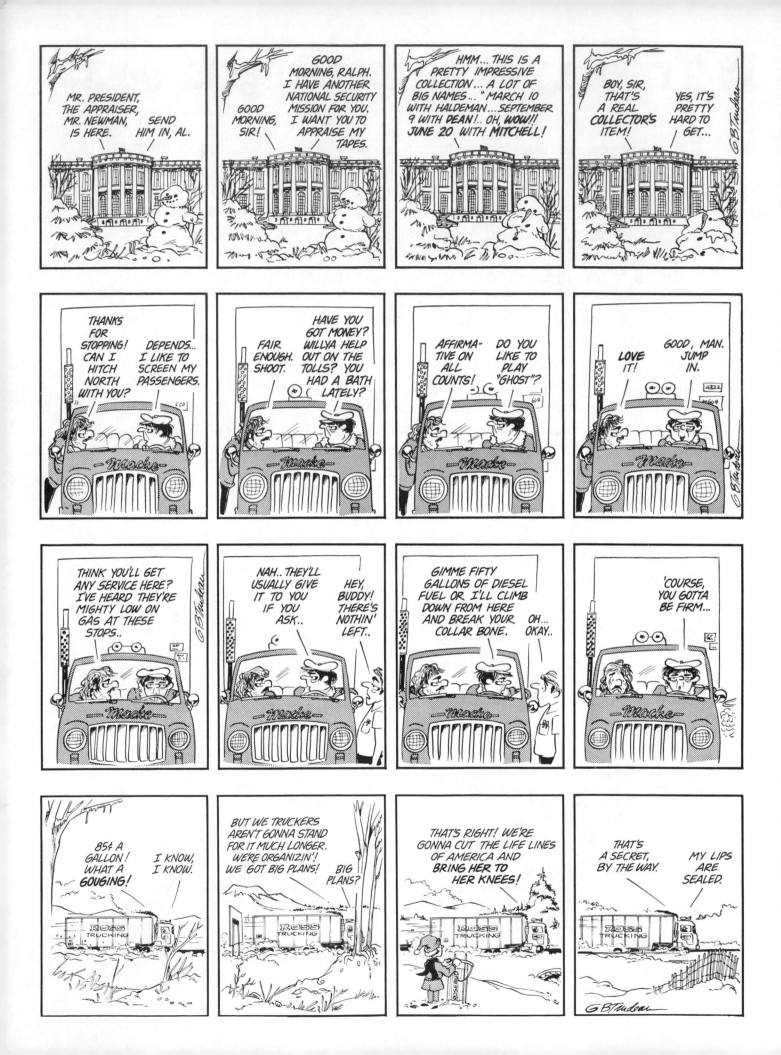

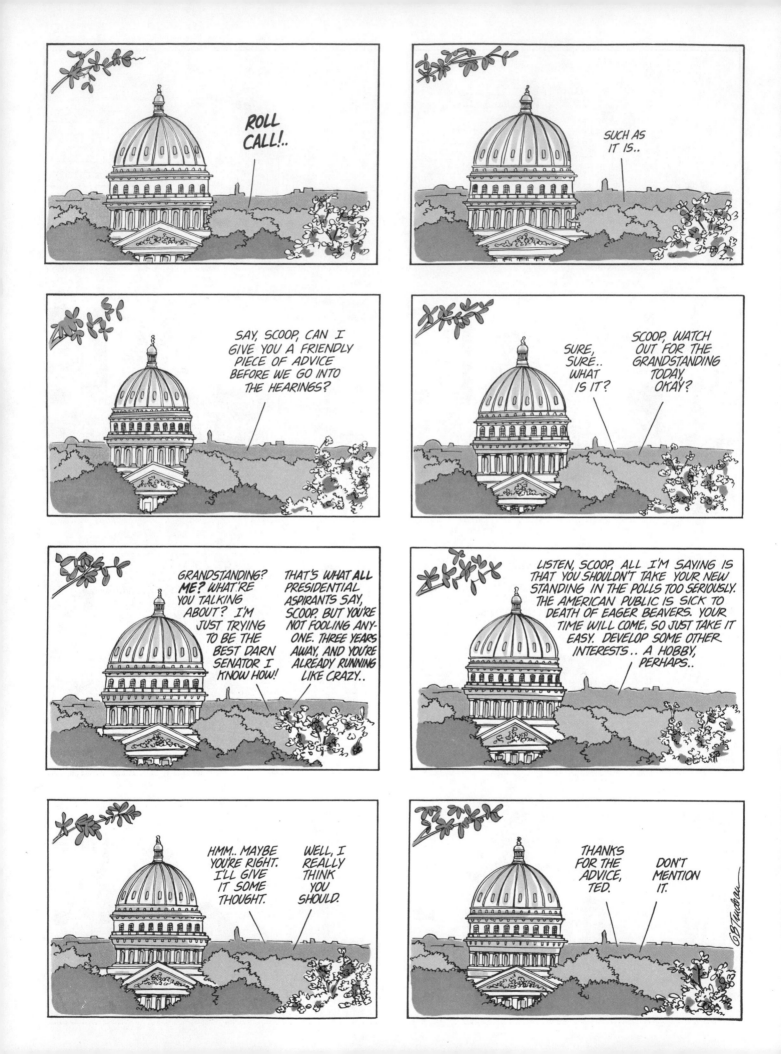

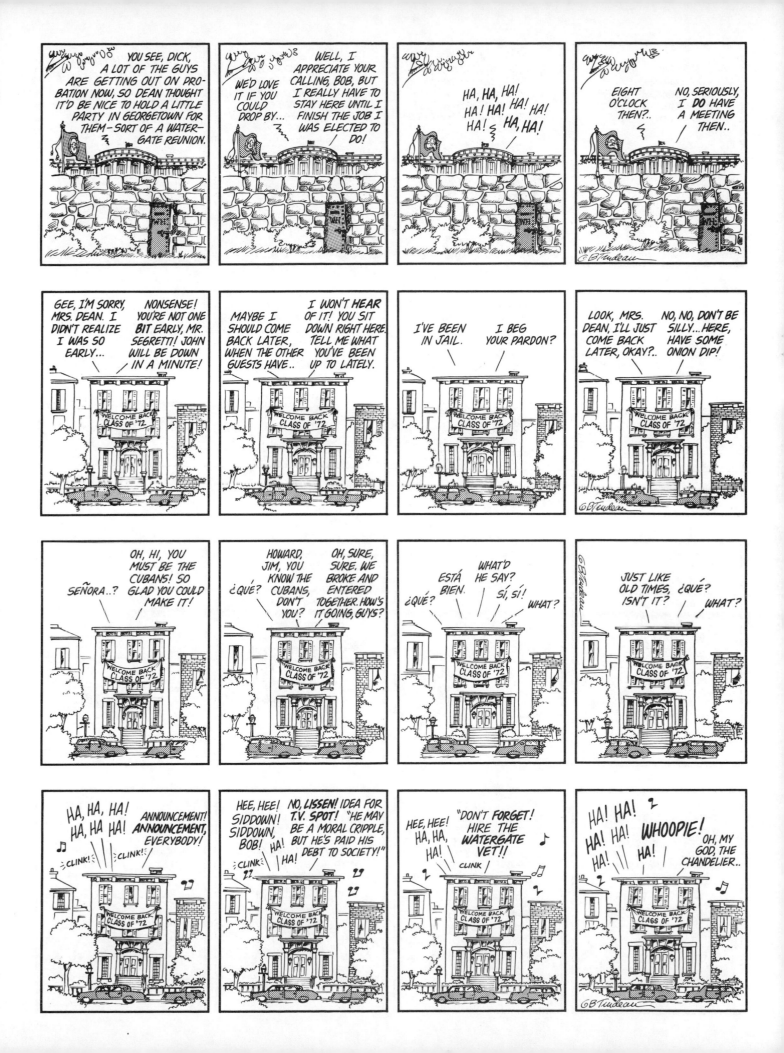

V/Brightening Up Our Tarnished Age

The crises break and the walls come down. Not only are the gates working again at the White House, but for this President even poolside isn't too chummy a milieu for meeting the press. And out at Berkeley, the new chumminess gets to Joanie, too, as she finds that having a right-on, law school roommate like Virginia means contending as well with her boyfriend, an improbable homebody named Clyde. If not all of the nation's wounds are healing—witness the lunchroom melee instigated by an eight-year-old participant of forced busing—things do seem to have settled down. And yet . . . Suppose we could get back to when it all started, or even imagine ourselves at Scot Sloan's publication party—with his cat Kent State, with the university president who remembers how it was, with all the gang playing their "best and brightest" roles. Have we come a long enough way to make sport of it all? Or should we wonder, with Mark and Mike, what happened to us?